I AM Always Taken Care Of

A New Age Guide to Overcoming Childhood Anxiety

Terry-Lee Pepin
Illustrated by Ayin Visitacion

To my Zoey,

My wish for you is that you know
You are never truly alone.

I have a present for you every day when you wake,
For as long as time stands, with you I will stay.

"I am safe"

My love for you is warmer than the sun,
And bigger than the moon.
Because I have a very important job to do,
And that's taking care of you!

"I am loved"

Today is a new day!
What makes you happy?
What makes your heart sing?
It's just like painting on a blank page,
YOU get to create your very own day!

"I am creative"

You can't see me with your eyes,
Or hear me with your ears,
But if you listen closely to your heart,
You will feel me near.

"I am light"

You can ask me anything!
You can tell me all your worries and fears,
And you will see, that by talking to me
They all disappear!

"I am brave"

It's okay to have many emotions,
Because that's how you learn and grow,
I am always holding your hand
Every step of the way,
So you'll never be alone!

"I am a warrior"

The day is almost done,
What fun we've had today.
It's time to close your eyes and think of something silly,
As you watch all your worries float away.

"I am peace"

When you wake tomorrow,
With you I will always stay.
I'll follow you as you lead the way,
Reminding you that today is always a good day!

Love always,
Your Guardian Angel

"I am always taken care of."

Download a free children's guided
meditation at the link below.

www.terryleepepin.com/iamalwaystakencareof

INTUITIVE GUIDE

About the Author

Terry-Lee is an international intuitive guide and medium. A mother to three beautiful souls, and a passion for learning that set forth an unshakable knowing and journey to help as many children as possible who suffer from anxiety. With the guidance, compassion and love from Spirit, Terry-Lee shares her messages with all parents that the answers to overcoming fear is love.

Balboa Press books may be ordered through booksellers or by contacting:

Balboa Press
A Division of Hay House
1663 Liberty Drive
Bloomington, IN 47403
www.balboapress.com
844-682-1282

Because of the dynamic nature of the Internet, any web addresses or links contained in this book may have changed since publication and may no longer be valid. The views expressed in this work are solely those of the author and do not necessarily reflect the views of the publisher, and the publisher hereby disclaims any responsibility for them.

Any people depicted in stock imagery provided by Getty Images are models, and such images are being used for illustrative purposes only.
Certain stock imagery © Getty Images.

ISBN: 978-1-9822-5340-0 (sc)
ISBN: 978-1-9822-5341-7 (e)

Library of Congress Control Number: 2020915868

Print information available on the last page.

Balboa Press rev. date: 08/31/2020

BALBOA.PRESS
A DIVISION OF HAY HOUSE

Printed in the United States
By Bookmasters